KNEBWORTH HOUSE

HERTFORDSHIRE HOME OF THE LYTTON FAMILY SINCE 1490

C000143295

Welcome to Knebworth

Lytton

Knebworth House and Park mean many things to many people. Here in the 21st Century Knebworth Park is best known worldwide as Britain's largest music venue, having hosted 18 major concerts since 1974, including the record-breaking weekend in 2003 when 375,000 people were entertained by Robbie Williams.

In the days before rock concerts Knebworth House was better known as the home of the Victorian novelist, playwright and politician, Edward Bulwer Lytton. Visit Knebworth in the 19th Century and you might expect to be entertained by Charles Dickens performing in the beautiful Jacobean Banqueting Hall.

The Hon. Henry Lytton Cobbold and his wife, Martha Lytton Cobbold

Music, literature and politics have featured throughout Knebworth's history. Edward's son, Robert Lytton, was both Viceroy of India and a popular romantic poet. Robert's daughter Constance was a militant suffragette and played an important part in winning the vote for women. Constance's niece, Hermione, married Cameron Cobbold, who became Governor of the Bank of England and Lord Chamberlain to the present Queen.

Every generation of the Lytton family has woven thread in the extraordinary tapestry of history that is represented here at Knebworth. As the 19th generation of the Lytton family to live in the house, my wife Martha and I invite you to join our extraordinary guest book that stretches all the way from Queen Elizabeth I to Queen Elizabeth II. Whether this is your first visit or you've visited us many times before... welcome to our home.

The Hon. Henry Lytton Cobbold

Cobbold

Contents

*One of the
angelic Heralds on
the Banqueting
Hall's chandelier*

THE HISTORY OF KNEBWORTH

The romantic exterior of Knebworth with its turrets, domes and gargoyles silhouetted against the sky does little to prepare the visitor for what to expect inside. The house has stood for many years longer than the 19th century decoration would suggest and the stucco hides from view a red brick house dating back to Tudor times.

Knebworth was probably first a Saxon settlement. The Domesday spelling in 1085 is '*Chenepeworde*', meaning '*village on the hill*'. Another more romantic interpretation is '*Cnebba's camp*' suggesting that Knebworth was formerly the home of Cnebba, the 5th century Saxon prince.

Edward the Confessor gave the Manor of Knebworth to his Thane Aschil. After the Conquest, the Manor and Fort were granted by William I to his favourite counsellor, Eudo Fitzherbert. During the intervening 400 years before the Lyttons acquired the estate, it was owned by many distinguished men, including Sir John Hotoft, Treasurer of the Household of Henry VI, who built the tower of St. Mary's Church in the park and was buried there in 1443. His daughter, Agnes, married Sir Robert de Lytton, Governor of Bolsover Castle and Grand Agister of the Forests of the Peak – the first connection between Knebworth and the Lyttons of Derbyshire.

On 17th February 1490, their grandson, Sir Robert Lytton, purchased Knebworth from his cousin's husband, Sir Thomas Bourchier, for £800. Sir Robert fought with Henry VII at Bosworth and became Under Treasurer to the Household and a close confidant.

Knebworth Hall 1500-1814

In about 1500, Sir Robert began to build onto the 15th century gatehouse a new four-sided house enclosing a central courtyard. Successive generations up to the present have moulded the house to their own highly individual requirements, building, demolishing, redecorating but, fortunately, never entirely obliterating the taste of a predecessor.

The house was described by Sir Henry Chaúncy in 1700 as *'a large pile of brick with a fair quadrangle in the middle of it, seated upon a dry hill, in a fair large park, stocked with the best deer in the country, excellent timber and well wooded and from thence you may behold a most lovely prospect to the East'*.

The House remained virtually unaltered until the 19th century; as late as 1805, the author of Excursion from Camerton to London and thence into Herts, was sufficiently impressed by Knebworth to place it after Haddon Hall as *'the most perfect specimen of the hospitable habitations of our ancestors which I have seen in the country'*.

However, the 'perfect specimen' was not destined to survive. In 1813, Mrs. Elizabeth Bulwer Lytton, finding the building 'old fashioned and too large', demolished three sides of the quadrangle, including the medieval gatehouse, part of which she re-erected as a lodge in the park. The principal changes to the remaining wing, put forward by her architect, John Biagio Rebecca, were the concealment of the red brick by stucco, the Gothicizing of the windows and the addition of eight towers, battlements and a porch.

Her son, the famous novelist, Sir Edward Bulwer Lytton, who succeeded her in 1843, went futher adding domes, turrets, gargoyles and stained glass and transforming the house into the gothic fantasy we know today. His extensive alterations were designed by H. E. Kendall, with interiors by John Crace and John Hardman who were, in the same period, working alongside Augustus Pugin on the Palace of Westminster. Pugin's influence is evident throughout the house, particularly in the State Drawing Room.

In 1881, Edward's son, Robert, 1st Earl of Lytton, commissioned architect John Lee to add a third storey to

part of the building, and architect George Devey added a Mock Tudor servants' wing at about the same time, which was demolished in 1949.

When the 2nd Earl, Victor, and his wife Pamela came to live at Knebworth in 1908, a new century had brought with it another change in taste and the gothic decoration was considered dark, fussy and old fashioned. They were fortunate in being able to seek advice from Victor's brother-in-law, soon to become the pre-eminent architect of his day, Sir Edwin Lutyens. Lutyens and Pamela were to form a happy partnership, each appreciating the other's taste, and until the end of his life Lutyens was to continue to advise on any alterations made in the house or garden.

But by the late 1940s Knebworth House was in a poor state of repair. Two World Wars, the Depression and taxes on the early deaths of two sons had taken their toll on the estate. Victor's daughter Hermione and her husband, Cameron 'Kim' Cobbold, moved into the southern end of the house in 1950, and took the decision to open the main rooms to the public on summer weekends.

Front view of Knebworth House in 1831

Courtesy of Hertfordshire Archives and Local Studies

Knebworth House after Edward Bulwer Lytton's alterations in the 1840s

Emergency repairs and dry rot eradication were carried out by selling chattels and estates properties, but it became increasingly clear that the restoration and long term maintenance of the house were beyond the means of the estate.

By the mid 1960s, Kim and Hermione, then Lord and Lady Cobbold, felt it would not be possible to continue family occupation of the house and efforts were made to find an appropriate institutional use for the building and grounds. The house had already been offered to the National Trust by Victor, the 2nd Earl, in the 1930s, but had been refused. Various institutions were approached, including a new University of Hertfordshire, but in each case the liability of maintaining the house ended discussions.

The next generation, however - inspired by 'stately home' pioneers at Woburn, Longleat and Beaulieu – set out to see if the house and gardens could be saved by exploiting the leisure potential of the park. In 1971, David Lytton Cobbold, and his wife Chryssie, opened up the park with a new entrance road from the A1(M) motorway and in one year visitor numbers jumped from 8,000 to 120,000.

Visitor numbers were further increased by establishing the park as the premier open air rock concert venue in the country.

David and Chryssie's efforts, again, enabled emergency repairs, but it was still clear that the long term future of the house was not secure. So, in 1984, the house was given by the family, on long lease, to a charitable trust, The Knebworth House Education and Preservation Trust. The Trust, presided over by heads of local government and members of the family, was able to raise an endowment with the support of the local authorities and, after 20 years of investment, has successfully completed a major restoration of the basic structure and external decoration of the northern end of the house and its central tower.

Since 2000, the house, park and estate have been managed by David and Chryssie's son Henry Lytton Cobbold and his wife Martha. They continue to fight for its preservation both by promoting Knebworth as a heritage and leisure venue, and by seeking to further endow the charitable trust so that it can finish its work in securing the future of this remarkable house.

KNEBWORTH'S LITERARY TRADITION

"Ladies and Gentlemen… You know very well that when the health, life and beauty now overflowing these halls shall have fled, crowds of people will come to see the place where he lived and wrote." Charles Dickens (speaking at Knebworth in 1865)

EDWARD BULWER LYTTON
(1803 – 1873)
(Andrew Brown ~ Academic Director, Cambridge University Press)

When Edward Bulwer Lytton died, in 1873, he was buried in Westminster Abbey and obituaries marked the passing of England's foremost man of letters. As early as 1834, two years after the death of Walter Scott, he had been hailed by the American Quarterly Review as *"without doubt, the most popular writer now living."*

Two decades later, in 1857, W.H. Smith reported that Bulwer Lytton was the most requested author at his railway station bookstalls. The pattern of success was to repeat itself right to the end of his career: of his novel A Strange Story (1861-2), which followed The Woman in White and Great Expectations as the principal serial in All the Year Round, The Times noted *"It appears to be the greatest of all the successes achieved by [the magazine]. Hundreds of thousands of readers rush to read… Sir E. B. Lytton."*

By any standards, Edward Bulwer Lytton's claims to literary fame were remarkable. During a career spanning five decades he

published two-dozen best-selling novels (including, in The Last Days of Pompeii, one of the most famous titles in all of nineteenth-century fiction); nine plays, two of which (Money and The Lady of Lyons) proved among the most resilient of the Victorian era; fifteen volumes of poetry, including an epic in twelve books (King Arthur) and

translations of Horace and Schiller; a history of Athens, a pioneering sociological survey of the national character (England and the English), four volumes of essays and enough uncollected prose to fill a dozen more. Samuel Smiles, the high-priest of Victorian industriousness, noted in 1859 that *"there are few living English writers who have written so much, and none that have produced so much of high quality."*

His general neglect today is well attested by his omission from the series of literary *"classics"* issued by Penguin and OUP (though located alphabetically in their lists between Charles Brockden Brown and Samuel Butler he would scarcely have been upstaged by his neighbours). Notwithstanding, there are clear signs of renascent academic interest in Bulwer Lytton as a new generation of scholars sets out to re-map the parameters of Victorian literary culture.

ROSINA BULWER LYTTON
(1802 – 1882)
(Marie Mulvey-Roberts ~ Reader in Literary Studies, University of the West of England, Bristol)

Rosina Doyle Wheeler was the younger daughter of the communitarian philosopher and campaigner for women's rights, Anna Wheeler, and Francis Massey Wheeler of Ballywire near Limerick in Ireland. Her wit, brilliance and beauty attracted the attention of Edward Bulwer Lytton, who proposed marriage in April 1826. Edward's mother, Mrs Bulwer, registered her strong disapproval of the marriage by cutting off her son's allowance, thus forcing him to earn his living from writing. The strain of his duel literary and political careers led him to neglect his wife and their two children Emily and Robert, born respectively in 1828 and in 1831, which eventually culminated in the collapse of their marriage. In 1836, they

'The pen is mightier than the sword'

Edward Bulwer Lytton (Richelieu Act II, Scene II)

separated acrimoniously and Edward later gained custody of the children. Now on a vastly decreased income, Rosina decided to follow his example by earning money through writing. Her first novel Cheveley: or The Man of Honour (1839), was a pointed attack on her husband, his circle, his family and Knebworth House itself, which she renamed Grimstone. To Bulwer Lytton's dismay, it was a best-seller, but to his consolation, it spawned a legion of enemies for Rosina, the most damaging of whom were members of the literary establishment.

Undaunted, Rosina went on to produce more provocative novels replaying the theme of the wronged wife, but she did not always confine her grievances to the pages of fiction. She threatened to sabotage Edward's play Not so Bad as We Seem by pelting the Guest of Honour, Queen Victoria, with oranges, and actually succeeded in disrupting an election meeting in Hertford to confirm his appointment as Colonial Secretary. Pushed to his limits, Edward tried to silence her by having her committed to a lunatic asylum, but within the month she was released, due to a public campaign waged on her behalf. Rosina wrote about her experiences in a memoir entitled A Blighted Life (1880). Edward's brother Henry summed up the feelings of the family by saying; 'She certainly is the very worst woman I ever heard of'.

After her death, Rosina was buried in an unmarked grave and her memory was hidden away in the family archives until the 1970s when her great-great-grandson David Lytton Cobbold hung her portrait in Knebworth House for the first time, named his daughter Rosina and, in 1995, erected a tombstone over her final resting place. For her defiance of social conventions which caused so many Victorian women to 'suffer and be silent', and for her polemic on behalf of the grievances of separated married women, Rosina Bulwer Lytton does indeed deserve to be remembered.

ROBERT BULWER LYTTON

(1831 – 1891)

(adapted from Owen Meredith by Aurelia Brooks Harlan)

The one enduring happy legacy of Edward and Rosina's marriage was their son Robert (their daughter Emily having died tragically of typhus aged 19). Robert's shining diplomatic career - culminating in the posts of Viceroy of India and British Ambassador to France - overshadows his critical success and popularity as a poet.

Given the choice Robert would have stuck solely to a literary career – it is said he would write his diplomatic dispatches first in

verse - but his father was adamant that a career in public service should come first. Publishing under the nom de plume "Owen Meredith" - to avoid being confused with his famous father – his early collections of poetry, such as The Wanderer (1858), were written under the influence of his friends Robert and Elizabeth Barrett Browning and caught the favourable wind of a resurgence of Byronism. His best-remembered work, a complete novel in verse entitled Lucile (1860), was for many new recruits to the reading class an introduction to verse that did not bore or bewilder.

"We may live without poetry, music and art;
We may live without conscience and live without heart;
We may live without friends; we may live without books;
But civilised man cannot live without cooks."

In England Lucile reached a fifth edition in 1893. In the United States its popularity was phenomenal, issuing from presses in ever-increasing numbers. Upwards of fifty publishers placed Lucile on their lists, and editions numbered more than a hundred. Had Lytton been protected by international copyright, he would have been able to enjoy the leisure for his art that he had longed for at the outset of his diplomatic career.

Instead his diplomatic life dominated, but throughout its trials – devastating famine in India, massacre and war in Afghanistan – Robert Lytton never stopped writing and he was writing poetry on the day he died, only two weeks after his sixtieth birthday.

"Talk not of genius baffled.
Genius is master of man.
Genius does what it must, and
Talent does what it can."

All five of his surviving children were published authors and many of his grandchildren, great- and great-great-grandchildren continue today to carry the Lytton literary torch.

LADY CONSTANCE LYTTON
AND THE SUFFRAGETTE MOVEMENT

Constance Lytton as Jane Warton, suffragette

Lady Constance Lytton, before throwing a stone at an MP's car at Newcastle, October 9th, 1909 and (below) later in life, wearing a suffragette medal.

Lady Constance Lytton (1869-1923), the second of Robert, 1st Earl of Lytton's three daughters, continued her grandmother Rosina and her great-grandmother Anna Wheeler's struggle for the emancipation of women.

In 1909, at the age of 39, she joined the Woman's Social and Political Union, the militant wing of Women's Suffrage Movement. Touring the country, giving speeches and trying to influence parliament, she also took part in stone throwing and was arrested and imprisoned four times. The first two times, she was released as soon as the authorities found out who she was, and that she had a brother in the House of Lords. The third time she disguised herself as a London seamstress named Jane Warton and was sentenced to two weeks hard labour in Walton Gaol, Liverpool. Here she went on hunger strike and like many of her fellow suffragettes suffered the horrors of forced feeding.

In 1910 an account of Constance's experiences was published in The Times, and by the time of her fourth imprisonment in 1911, suffragettes were being treated as political prisoners and conditions were improved. Her ordeal, however, had seriously affected her health and, suffering a series of strokes, she was left paralysed down the right side of her body. Undaunted, she wrote, with her left hand, her own account of her ordeal, Prisons and Prisoners (1914), which became widely read and influential in prison reform.

She never fully regained her strength and died aged only 54, but not before Parliament had passed a bill, in January 1918, giving women the vote. Inscribed on the mausoleum in Knebworth Park, her family has left the following epitaph, "Endowed with a celestial sense of humour, boundless sympathy, and rare musical talent, she devoted the later years of her life to the political enfranchisement of women and sacrificed her health and talents in helping to bring victory to this cause".

"In years to come this story of compassion and chivalry will be told in the schools to children yet unborn… And many a woman child will say in her heart: 'I, too, will be fearless and chivalrous and brave.'"

(Katherine Roberts, writing about Constance Lytton, in "Page in the Diary of a Militant Suffragette" 1910)

THE COBBOLDS

The Cobbolds have for many centuries been a Suffolk family, probably of Saxon origin. There is an old Saxon word 'Kobold', meaning a goblin and especially associated with mines – hence the mineral cobalt.

The earliest record is of a John Cobbold of Suffolk in 1274. Since the early 18th century the Cobbolds have been brewers and bankers in Ipswich. In the nineteenth century the Cobbolds were exceptionally prolific: John Cobbold, who died in 1835, married twice and produced 22 children. His eldest son and grandson, both John, produced respectively 14 and 13. The ninth of the 13 was Nathaniel Fromanteel, grandfather of the 1st Lord Cobbold.

Nathaniel's mother was a granddaughter of Martha Fromanteel, the last of the famous clockmaking family who came from Holland as refugees in the reign of Elizabeth I. Ahasueras Fromanteel was the first to construct a pendulum clock in England in 1658. As Master of the Worshipful Company of Clockmakers, he was one of the earliest subscribers to the Bank of England.

Cameron 'Kim', 1st Lord Cobbold

Nathaniel Cobbold ran the family banking business of Bacon, Cobbold and Company in Ipswich, which was founded in 1786, and is now absorbed within Lloyds Bank. It was Nathaniel's mother's wish that all his male descendants should, like him, bear the name Fromanteel, a wish that has been followed to the present day. His elder son, Clement Fromanteel, was a barrister, a Lieutenant Colonel in the Suffolk Regiment during the First World War and later secretary of the Royal Cancer Hospital. Clement's elder son, Cameron Fromanteel, married Lady Hermione Bulwer Lytton, who inherited Knebworth from her father.

'Kim' Cobbold, as he was known by all, joined the Bank of England in 1933 and was Governor from 1949 to 1961. For his services to the Bank of England, he was created Baron Cobbold of Knebworth in 1960. From 1963 to 1971 he was Lord Chamberlain of Her Majesty's Household. He was made a Privy Councillor in 1959 and Knight of the Garter in 1970. Lord Cobbold died in 1987 and was succeeded by his eldest son, David Antony Fromanteel, also a banker and corporate treasurer. David, his wife, Chryssie, and their four children, Henry, Peter, Richard and Rosina, and two informal foster children, Danny and Harry Matovu lived at Knebworth House from 1971 until 2000.

David, 2nd Lord Cobbold, takes part in a mediaeval jousting tournament in 2005

Sir Robert Lytton

Sir Rowland Lytton

Sir William Lytton

Sir William Lytton

William Robinson-Lytton

John Robinson-Lytton

Richard Warburton-Lytton

Elizabeth Warburton-Lytton

Edward Bulwer Lytton

Robert, 1st Earl of Lytton

Victor, 2nd Earl of Lytton

Lady Hermione
Bulwer Lytton

David & Chryssie,
Lord & Lady Cobbold

Henry, Martha
and family

THE LYTTONS
OF KNEBWORTH

Sir Robert Lytton = Elizabeth Andrews
d.1504

William de Lytton = Audrey Booth

Frances = Sir Robert Lytton = Elizabeth
Cavalery   d.1551   Munden

Margaret = Rowland Lytton = Anne
Tate   d. 1582   Carleton

Sir Rowland Lytton = Anne St. John
1561-1615

Sir Anthony Cope Bt. = Frances

Anne Slaney = Sir William Lytton = Ruth Barrington
              1589-1660

Judith Edwards = Sir Rowland Lytton = Rebecca Chapman
                 1615-1674

Mary Harrison = Sir William Lytton = Philippa Kelyng
                1643-1705

Judith = Sir Nicholas Strode
1639 - 1662

Col. John Robinson of Gwersyllt = Margaret Morris
1616 - 1681

Wm. Robinson = Anne Myddelton

Margaret Robinson = Sir George Strode
                    d. 1707

William Robinson-Lytton = Elizabeth Heysham
d. 1732

Lytton Strode Lytton = Bridget Mostyn
d.1710

John Robinson-Lytton = Leonora Brereton
1724 - 1762

Barbara = William Warburton
b. 1710

Richard Warburton-Lytton = Elizabeth Jodrell
1745 - 1810

Elizabeth Warburton-Lytton = General William Earle Bulwer
1773 - 1843

Edward Bulwer Lytton, 1st Lord Lytton = Rosina Wheeler
1803 - 1873

Robert, 1st Earl of Lytton = Edith Villiers
1831 - 1891

Victor, 2nd Earl of Lytton, K.G. = Pamela Chichele-Plowden
1876 - 1947

Lady Hermione Bulwer Lytton = Cameron Fromanteel Cobbold, 1st Lord Cobbold, K.G.
1905 - 2004   1904 - 1987

David Lytton Cobbold, 2nd Lord Cobbold = Christine Stucley
b. 1937   b. 1940

Henry Lytton Cobbold = Martha Boone
b. 1962   b. 1964

Morwenna   Edward
b. 1989   b. 1992

THE ENTRANCE HALL &
THE PICTURE GALLERY

The Entrance Hall was given its present form by Sir Edwin Lutyens in the early years of the 20th century. Immediately on the right is the Picture Gallery, containing 17th and 18th century portraits. The far end of the room was the original kitchen of the Tudor house.

Redesigned in the late 1920s, it is now a Drawing Room linking the public and private sides of the house and often used by the family.

In the Entrance Hall, Armoury and Banqueting Hall, note the set of sixteen hall chairs, unusual in their high-back design and grisaille decoration, the oldest of which dates from the early 18th century. The wooden statues of Diana and Ceres, the one with her hound, the other with her cornucopia, are of Bohemian early 18th century workmanship. The two embroidered and painted hangings are also 18th century, German, and were formerly entrance curtains to the Banqueting Hall.

The Picture Gallery

A detail of the 1st Lord Cobbold's Garter Banner

BANQUETING HALL

The Banqueting Hall has been the focal point of family occupation of Knebworth House for over five centuries. Like much of the house, it is a splendid blend of the many changes in public taste that have taken place in England over this period.

Sir Robert Lytton

The stone floor with no cellar beneath suggests earlier origins, but the present hall dates from the rebuilding work of the 1560s and is typical of a traditional great hall of an English Tudor or Elizabethan house. The great oak screen at the entrance was installed by Sir Rowland Lytton in the early 1600s and is a perfect example of the native style. The paneling on the three remaining walls dates from a century later, and follows Inigo Jones' discovery of Palladio and the consequent Classical revival. In the 19th Century, this wood was dark-stained by Sir Edward Bulwer Lytton and the room decorated with heraldic symbols, banners and suits of armour. In the early 20th century, Sir Edwin Lutyens removed some of this gothic grandeur and the room now blends baronial splendour with the natural woodwork and clean lines of earlier periods.

Sir Rowland Lytton

At the far end of the hall is a portrait of Sir Robert Lytton, the first member of the Lytton family to live at Knebworth. On the right of the fireplace is Sir Rowland Lytton, his great-grandson, aged 25, in one of the finest surviving paintings of the period.

In 1850, the Banqueting Hall served as a theatre when Charles Dickens and his celebrated troupe of amateur actors performed three private productions of Ben Jonson's *Every Man In His Humour*. To provide music for the performance, Dickens hired a huge hybrid musical instrument called a '*choremusicon*', which he assured would be "*better than three musicians*", but which required one of the windows to be removed for it to be hoisted into the hall. "*Everything*", Dickens wrote afterwards to a friend, "*has gone off in a whirl of triumph, and fired the whole length and breadth of the county of Hertfordshire.*"

Read the rede of this old roof tree
Here be trust safe, opinion free,
Knightly right-hand, Christian knee,
Worth in all, wit in some,
Laughter open, slander dumb.
Hearth where rooted friendships grow
Safe as altar even to foe
Home where chivalry and grace
Cradle a high-hearted race.
If thy sap in these may be
Fear no winter, old roof tree.

Edward Bulwer Lytton's words of welcome
around the frieze of the Banqueting Hall

During the 1930s Winston Churchill, a frequent guest of Victor, 2nd Earl of Lytton and his wife, Pamela, sat here at his easel. His painting of the Banqueting Hall (above), hangs below the portrait of Sir Robert Lytton.

Above Sir Robert's portrait hangs the Garter Banner of Cameron Fromanteel Cobbold, 1st Lord Cobbold, Governor of the Bank of England, Lord Chamberlain to Queen Elizabeth II and Knight of the Garter, who died in 1987.

Edward Bulwer Lytton in the entrance to the Banqueting Hall c. 1855

THE DINING PARLOUR

*Known as the Oak Room
in Victorian times and as the
White Drawing Room after 1908,
when it was transformed by
Pamela, Countess of Lytton,
and Edwin Lutyens, the room is once
again a dining parlour as it was in the
original Tudor house.*

The red velvet and silver embroidery on the two sofas and six chairs is Jacobean and said to be from James I's state bedroom at Wanstead House, Essex. The 12 dining chairs with their barley-twist frames date from the mid-19th century and are of applewood. The dining table is rosewood banded with satinwood and of the late Georgian period. The dinner service is mid-18th century from the Royal factory of Berlin. Monogramed 'L.B.', the service was acquired by Edward Bulwer Lytton when his name – before inheriting the Lytton estate – was still Edward Lytton Bulwer.

*The Dining
Parlour table set
with the Berlin
dinner service and
Venetian glass*

The glass is Venetian and bears the Lytton coat of arms. It was made for Robert, 1st Earl of Lytton, when he was appointed Viceroy of India. It has twice travelled by sea to India, with Robert in the 1870s and with Victor, his son, in the 1920s.

The tortoiseshell and ivory cabinets date from the late 17th century and are thought to be Indo Portuguese, probably from Goa. The cabinet veneered with tortoiseshell and framed with ebony and ormolu is 17th century Flemish.

The paintings are all family portraits. Perhaps the finest is the portrait by Sir Peter Lely of Ruth, daughter of Sir Francis Barrington and a first cousin of Oliver Cromwell. She married Sir William Lytton, an active Parliamentarian who led the Hertfordshire opposition to Charles I's illegal imposition of Ship Money and was imprisoned in Pride's Purge in 1648.

In the early 18th century, Knebworth passed by marriage to the Robinson family. By contrast, the Robinsons were staunch Royalists. Colonel John Robinson, of Gwersyllt, Denbighshire, had been a commander in Charles I's forces in North Wales.

The Oak Drawing Room, 19th century

The White Drawing Room, 20th century

Pictured is Natasha, wife of Archduke Michael Romanov, who was to become the last Tzar of Russia. Michael and Natasha rented Knebworth House in 1913, for what was to be the happiest year of their troubled and short life together.

The Parliamentarian and the Royalist: Ruth, Lady Lytton, by Sir Peter Lely and Colonel John Robertson by van Hoogstraeten (far right)

THE LIBRARY

This is the room that Edward Bulwer Lytton, novelist, playwright and Member of Parliament, made into his Library when he succeeded to Knebworth in 1843.

"*My grandfather had left debts to be defrayed. Everyone, Heaven knows, who comes into possession of an estate long neglected, and a great country house half tumbling down, wants ready money to begin with. So my mother sold my grandfather's library.*" Prior to its sale, Richard Warburton-Lytton's extensive and scholarly library had a profound effect on his 8-year-old grandson, Edward. "*Behold the great event of my infant life – my Siege of Troy, my Persian Invasion, my Gallic Revolution – the Arrival of my Grandfather's Books!*"

"Out of the classical works in dead languages, my mother only reserved one, "Lives of the Philosophers" by Diogenes Laertius… (to be) settled as an heirloom on the future owners of Knebworth. Probably my mother had a subtle and wise notion that a man plagued with a property in land had need make acquaintance with philosophers."

In rebuilding a library worthy of his grandfather, Bulwer Lytton made a major contribution with his own work. He wrote 70 volumes of novels, plays, poems and essays, all of which are represented in the Library in various editions.

His son, Robert Bulwer Lytton, continued the family's contribution to the collection, writing several volumes of poetry under the nom de plume "Owen Meredith", so as not to be confused with his illustrious father. The distinction was to be made clearer when Robert was created 1st Earl of Lytton by Queen Victoria for his distinguished diplomatic career, specifically as Viceroy of India (1877-1880), a post conferred on him by his father's old friend and fellow author, the Prime Minister, Benjamin Disraeli.

A sketch of Robert as a young man by G. F. Watts hangs above the fireplace; the finished portrait is in the National Portrait Gallery. The marble roundel set into the Lutyens fireplace shows him in his later years and was made by Sir Alfred Gilbert as a model for his memorial in St. Paul's Cathedral. The motto above the fireplace is a quotation from Virgil, referring to the surrounding bookshelves, *"Hic Vivunt Vivere Digni"* (*"Here live they that are worthy to live"*).

Robert's son, Victor, the 2nd Earl of Lytton, was married in 1902 to the great beauty, Pamela Plowden. Pamela had been brought up in India and was the first love of Winston Churchill. Amongst the heirlooms on display in the Library is one of the many letters sent by Winston to Pamela during their lifelong friendship. It was Pamela who, together with her brother-in-law Edwin Lutyens, has such a defining influence on the redecoration of the house in the Edwardian period.

Victor, 2nd Earl of Lytton and Winston Churchill in 1910

Pamela Plowden in India where she first met Winston Churchill

ARMOURY AND STAIRCASE

The Staircase dates from 1844 and is the creation of Sir Edward Bulwer Lytton working with his architect, H E Kendall and his designer, John Crace.

Very little has changed since Bulwer Lytton's day. The double flight of oak stairs surmounted by lions bearing armorial shields and a magnificent pair of Nubian figures has remained much as he knew it. The two long mullion windows contain family coats of arms in stained glass by John Hardman; the decorative motif of the oak leaf (lei) and the cask (tun) is a punning reference to the name Lytton.

Between the windows hangs the Garter banner of Victor, 2nd Earl of Lytton, statesman and man of letters. He was a champion of women's suffrage, a pioneer in the establishment of the National Theatre and a strong supporter of the League of Nations, where he was leader of the Indian Delegation 1927–28, British Delegate 1931 and Chairman of the League's Commission on Manchuria in 1932. Victor was born in India and returned as Governor of Bengal 1922–27. He was acting Viceroy for four months in 1925. The portrait of him in Garter robes (opposite) which hangs at the foot of the stairs was painted by his younger brother, Neville, a professional artist who lived mostly in Paris and who is also represented in a delightful self portrait (left).

Cameron and Hermione Cobbold in the Oak Study of Knebworth House by Edward Halliday (1956)

Cameron, 1st Lord Cobbold painted posthumously by Julia Heseltine in 1990

Following the early death of Victor's two sons, Neville Lytton succeeded his brother in 1947 as 3rd Earl of Lytton, but Victor left Knebworth House to his daughter, Hermione, who married Cameron Fromanteel, 1st Lord Cobbold. Neville's grandson, John, is now 5th Earl of Lytton and lives in Sussex.

At the top of each flight are portraits of Cameron "Kim" Cobbold: one with his wife Hermione, and their beloved Labradors that were to become part of the Cobbold coat of arms when Kim was made the 1st Lord Cobbold in 1960 for his services to the Bank of England; and one in his Knight of the Garter robes (awarded in 1970) with his grandson Richard, who was page to the Queen in 1980–81.

Note the exposed patch of brickwork on the Armoury wall. This shows the original Tudor red brick exterior wall and the stone mullions of the Banqueting Hall windows that existed prior to the addition of this extension in the late 17th century.

The armour surrounding it and at the foot of the stairs was collected by Bulwer Lytton to create an atmosphere of romantic antiquity. It dates from various periods but the majority is from the 17th century.

Above the staircase hangs a romantic portrait of Bulwer Lytton as a young man painted by Gustav Von Holst.

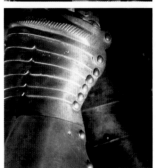

STAIRCASE LANDING

Surrounding mementos from the life and career of Edward Bulwer Lytton are portraits of his wife, Rosina, and children, Emily and Robert. The literary and political success that Bulwer Lytton enjoyed was won at the expense of his family life.

Rosina Bulwer
by A E Chalon

Robert

Emily

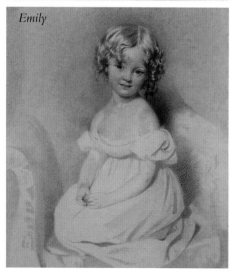

"Years have passed since I experienced any emotion like that which I feel for you at this moment. Better perhaps for me if I had still been successful in subduing my heart…"

Better indeed! For ten years after writing these words on first meeting the fiery Irish beauty Rosina Wheeler, Edward Bulwer was signing a Deed of Separation to end their disastrous relationship. The couple continued to harass each other for another forty years. In 1958 Rosina was committed to a lunatic asylum for publicly denouncing her husband in Hertford as he sought confirmation of his appointment as Colonial Secretary in Lord Derby's government:

"Men of Herts, if you have the hearts of men, hear me! How can the people of England submit to have such a man at the head of the Colonies, who ought to have been in the Colonies as a transport long ago!"

The only positive legacy of the Bulwers' relationship was their two children, Emily (b. 1828) and Robert (b. 1831), but there was tragedy in their story too. Emily, having been abandoned during her teenage years to a German medical institution to correct curvature of the spine, died alone in a London boarding house aged 19, officially of typhus, but ultimately of a broken heart. Her brother Robert, 16 at the time, later wrote the following words:

> **"She pass'd out of my youth at the still time**
> **O' the early light, when all was green and husht.**
> **She pass'd, and pass'd away. Like broken rhyme**
> **Her sweet short life's few relics are. This crusht**
> **And scatter'd rose, she dropp'd; that page she turn'd,**
> **And finished not; this curl, her gift; this knot**
> **That flutter'd from her… Hard world, harm them not!**
> **My right to keep them hath been sorely earn'd."**

THE OVAL ANTE-ROOM

It was in the Oval Room that Sir Rowland Lytton, depicted in the ceiling painting (right), greeted Queen Elizabeth I on her visit to Knebworth in 1571.

It now contains paintings of the Bulwer family, including Edward Bulwer Lytton's two elder brothers, William, who inherited the Bulwer estates at Heydon in Norfolk, and Henry, later Lord Dalling, diplomat and biographer of Lord Palmerston.

William and Henry Bulwer, two elder brothers of Edward Bulwer Lytton, as children

THE STATE DRAWING ROOM

This is one of the finest surviving examples of early Victorian interior decoration and a perfect embodiment of that revival of interest in the High Gothic.

The room was originally called the Presence Chamber and led into the Long Gallery that was demolished in 1811. When Edward Bulwer inherited Knebworth from his mother Elizabeth Bulwer Lytton in 1843, he commissioned John Crace (then very much under the influence of Augustus Pugin) to redesign the room to reflect her illustrious Lytton ancestry: the ceiling represents her forty-four armorial quarterings; the frieze depicts the arms of families through which she derived her descent from King Edward III and the legendary 7th century Welsh king, Cadwallader; and the stained glass window contains a full-length portrait of her ancestors' most prized patron, the first Tudor King, Henry VII.

North-facing, and until recently without radiators, this magnificent room escaped redecoration by Lutyens and the Edwardians partly because it was too cold to live in.

The painting to the right of the fireplace is one of the great history paintings executed by Daniel Maclise and represents Caxton's printing press. It was painted in 1850, when Maclise wrote to Bulwer Lytton: 'I have derived every idea I required as to my personages from The Last of the Barons.' This was one of Bulwer Lytton's best-known books; the novelist himself appears in the painting, in armour, as Lord Rivers.

Saducismus Triumphatus:

OR,

Full and Plain EVIDENCE
Concerning

WITCHES
AND
APPARITIONS.

In Two Parts.
The First treating of their
POSSIBILITY,
The Second of their Real
EXISTENCE.

By *Joseph Glanvil* late Chaplain in Ordinary to
his Majesty, and Fellow of the Royal Society.

With a Letter of Dr. HENRY MORE
on the same Subject.

And an Authentick, but wonderful story of certain *Swedish* Witches; done into English by *Anth. Horneck*,
Preacher at the *Savoy*.

LONDON; Printed for *J. Collins* at his Shop under the Temple-
Church, and *S. Lownds* at his Shop by the *Savoy-gate*, 1681.

BULWER LYTTON'S STUDY

Collected in the room in which he wrote are many of the personal effects, manuscripts and influences of the man whom the 1859 Encyclopedia Brittanica judged as "now unquestionably the greatest living novelist of England."

The table cloth is the same, if a little worn; the sealing wax holder is the same, if without its sealing wax; the beaded tapestries are the same, if hung a little lower; but if Edward Bulwer Lytton was still sitting at this table, as he is in E. M. Ward's 1854 portrait above the fireplace, he would now be over 200 years old.

His distinctive long cherry-wood pipes are still here. *"A pipe,"* he says in Night and Morning, *"it is a great soother – a pleasant comforter. Blue devils fly before its honest breath. It ripens the brain: it opens the heart and the man who smokes, thinks like a sage and acts like a Samaritan."*

Opposite: A collection of items belonging to Bulwer Lytton including two skulls excavated from Pompeii

Bulwer Lytton's crystal ball   *Ceiling detail*   *Bronze lamp*

Like some of his tastes, much of his work is now out of fashion, but a collection put together for his Bicentenary in 2003 reveals many of the ways in which he still touches our lives: there are the *"Lytton"* and *"Bulwer"* town and street names in British Columbia, Canada, and Queensland, Australia, territories that were named when he was Secretary for the Colonies; there are the constant use in journalism and popular culture of his words, *"The pen is mightier than the sword"* and *"It was a dark and stormy night"*; there are the many film and television adaptations of his work, especially The Last Days of Pompeii; there are the numerous musical compositions inspired by his work, notably Richard Wagner's breakthrough opera Rienzi; there is even the sandwich spread and soup stock Bovril, which was named after the energy source *"vril"* from his science fiction novel The Coming Race.

The manuscript of his 1838 comedy Money, which was recently revived by the National Theatre, is on display; as are letters from Charles Dickens about Bulwer Lytton's suggestion of a happy ending for Great Expectations, and their joint creation of the Guild of Literature and Art, a benevolent fund for struggling writers and artists, for which Bulwer Lytton wrote the play *"Not So Bad As We Seem"* for Dickens to take on tour in aid of the charity.

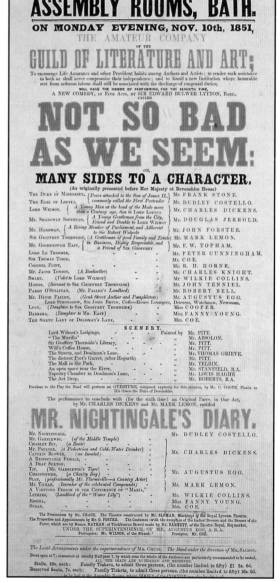

The playbill for 'Not So Bad As We Seem'

The Banqueting Hall in 1850, showing the Minstrels' Gallery

MINSTRELS' GALLERY

*From the Minstrels' Gallery the visitor has a spectacular view of the Banqueting Hall
and of the carved wooden bosses of Sir Rowland Lytton's oak ceiling timbers.
The frieze poem was written by Bulwer Lytton and starts in the far corner of the gallery.*

On the wall are two curiosities that span 500 years of Lytton family history: a framed manuscript order addressed to Sir Robert Lytton and signed by Henry VII for new shoes for the princes and princesses – including the young Henry VIII; and a framed cheque for £684,149,248, a British Petroleum tax return relating to the Forties Field in March 1983, then the largest sterling cheque ever written, and signed by David Lytton Cobbold, the company's then Treasury Manager.

A collection of early ski clothes and equipment evokes the origins of winter sports. The Lyttons were among the pioneers of skiing for pleasure. Antony, elder son of Victor, the 2nd Earl of Lytton, won the Kandahar Cup in Murren, Switzerland, in 1924 and wrote to his father, *"My God, I did come a pace down that valley. I have never been so scared! I don't think anyone has ever had such fast skis before."*

THE FALKLAND ROOM

The first of the bedrooms is named after Rebecca, Viscountess Falkland, daughter of Sir Rowland Lytton (1615-1674) and wife of the 5th Viscount Falkland. Her portrait hangs above the fireplace.

The room is hung with hand-painted Chinese wallpaper of the early 1900s. The little pagoda (right), was Charles Dickens' inspiration for '*the Chinese house for Jip with little bells on the top*' which Dora and David Copperfield bought for her dog instead of the more practical fender and meat screen. '*It takes a long time to accustom Jip to his new residence, after we have bought it; whenever he goes in or out, he makes the little bells ring, and is horribly frightened.*'

The Chinese bronze Ting (cauldron for meats and grains), dates from the late Chou period (*c.*500 B.C.) and was presented in 1932 to Victor, 2nd Earl of Lytton, by the Chinese Government in gratitude for his work as Chairman of the League of Nations Manchurian Commission which produced the '*Lytton Report*'.

The Dresden dog is a model, supposedly life-size, of the Empress Catherine's favourite lap-dog. It is thought to have been a gift from Archduke Michael and Natasha Romanov

Opposite: The room is dominated by this traditional bridal bed, which would have been given by the groom's parents. It is constructed from seperate panels, which enabled it to be dismantled and moved easily

The Hampden Room

Named after John Hampden, leader of the
Parliamentary cause who, tradition has it, visited
Sir William Lytton at Knebworth, this room was
later the childhood bedroom of Edward Bulwer
Lytton, next to that of his mother.

*An early edition of
Winnie the Pooh signed by both
A A Milne and Christopher Robin Milne*

Hermione as a child

the forward, *"I have never heard a more glorious laugh in man or boy; it overfilled him: I think he laughed last in his last moment, or one prefers to believe his laugh accompanies him still."*

Hermione's younger brother, John, who succeeded Antony as Viscount Knebworth, was killed leading his squadron in the great tank battle of El Alamein in 1942, which proved a decisive turning point in World War II. Winston Churchill ended a letter of condolence to his mother, *"Let us thank God that after its fearful peril England – for whom all may be offered – stands safe and glorious, and that its heroes have not given their lives without a purpose being fulfilled. I am sure dearest that you will now be able to survey the whole scene of our lives from a high place, and that the glory of bringing*

John, Viscount Knebworth, while fighting in the desert

such men as Antony and John into the world, and the joy of sharing and shaping their childhood and youth, will outshine the agony of shattered hopes and bitter separation."

This room is now used to display the family's collection of children's furniture, toys and books. The large and much loved Steiff bear and the doll's house belonged to Hermione, daughter of Victor, 2nd Earl of Lytton's. *"The doll's house,"* she recalled, *"had belonged to my aunt. I remember my brother and I thought it wasn't a proper house as it had no staircase."*

Hermione inherited Knebworth on her father's death in 1947 because her two brothers, tragically, predeceased him. Antony, Viscount Knebworth, who's childhood Napoleon suit is seen here, was killed practicing a formation dive for the annual Hendon Air Display in 1933. His life was commemorated by his father in Antony: A Record of Youth (1935), which was widely read throughout the English-speaking world. J.M. Barrie, godfather to Antony's best friend Nico Llewellyn Davies wrote in

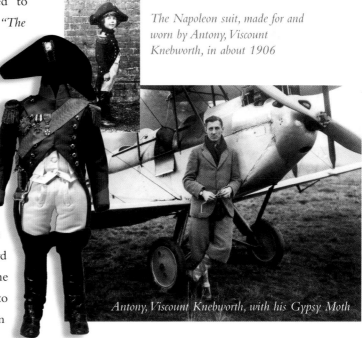

The Napoleon suit, made for and worn by Antony, Viscount Knebworth, in about 1906

Antony, Viscount Knebworth, with his Gypsy Moth

MRS BULWER LYTTON'S ROOM

This was the bedroom used by Elizabeth Bulwer Lytton during her tenure of Knebworth, from 1811 to 1843. As requested by her son, in an inscription over the fireplace, it remains very much the room she knew.

Elizabeth inherited Knebworth from her father, the scholar, Richard Warburton-Lytton. He had preferred to live by the sea at Ramsgate than in *"the old half-feudal pile"* with its *"gloomy courtyard"* and *"melancholy neglected park"*, as his grandson Edward described Knebworth at first sight.

Elizabeth's married life was spent at her husband, General William Earle Bulwer's, property at Heydon Hall in Norfolk. Following his death in 1807, and her father's in

Behind Mrs Bulwer Lytton's late 18th century mantlepiece clock are Edward Bulwer Lytton's instructions to his descendants.

1810, she moved to Knebworth with her third and favourite son, Edward, then aged 8, and added the ancestral name *"Lytton"* to her married name.

Mrs Bulwer Lytton was a formidable character, reminiscent of dowagers from the pages of Jane Austen. She quarreled with every rector, primarily about the tithe that the church claimed on all estate produce. The rectors were left preaching to empty churches when she insisted that her staff and tenants attend alternative services that she held in the house's State Drawing Room. For these she used the large bible now at the foot of her bed, dated 1827, and bearing her initials EBBL (Elizabeth Barbara Bulwer Lytton). So that she and her family would not have to be buried at the church - which she screened from the house with plantings - she commissioned a mausoleum in the park, in which she now rests alongside many of her descendants.

Indicative of the room's Regency style is the false door to the right of the bed, of no other purpose than symmetry. The painting and drawings all belonged to Elizabeth; some are in her own hand, including two pictures of her favourite dog, an Italian pug named Juba. One reads, *"This picture is to commemorate extraordinary canine sagacity, fidelity and attachment, July 1821."*

Mrs Bulwer Lytton's Pug dog 'Juba'

Some necessary changes have been made to the room, including the recent replacement of the Aubusson carpet in an exact copy of the original design.

Mrs Bulwer Lytton
as a child being held
by her mother,
by Daniel Gardner

This room long occupied by Elizabeth Bulwer Lytton and
containing the relics most associated with her memory.
Her son trusts that her descendants will preserve unaltered -
'*LIBERIS VIRTUTIS EXEMPLAR*'

THE QUEEN ELIZABETH ROOM

Edward Bulwer Lytton's inscription over the fireplace in this room commemorates a visit to Knebworth by Queen Elizabeth I in 1588, the year of the Armada, to thank Sir Rowland Lytton for assembling the Hertfordshire county militia at Tilbury to meet the Spanish threat on land.

There is no proof of a visit in 1588, but evidence has recently come to light of a four-day visit by the Queen in 1571. Copies of two royal accounts relating to the visit are displayed in the room. Having the Queen to stay was an expensive business, known occasionally to bankrupt estates, but Sir Rowland was later rewarded with the coveted position of Captain of the Queen's Band of Pensioners.

Whether this is the actual bedroom the Queen used is not certain, but since 1811 at least, it has been the house's main guest room and slept in by many celebrated friends and acquaintances of the family. More recent guests include Mick Jagger, when the Rolling Stones played at Knebworth in 1976, and Noel Gallagher, who had a bath in the adjoining bathroom when Oasis played Knebworth in 1996.

What is certain is that the Queen did not sleep in the oak four-poster bed. Despite its Tudor style, this was made in the early 19th century out of pieces of older beds. The wall panels are Jacobean, depicting scenes from the Bible.

The plaster ceiling is a 20th century addition by Victor, 2nd Earl of Lytton.

Many of the paintings, however, may well have been enjoyed by the Queen. When, after the Reformation, images were forbidden in English churches, painters lost not only their subject matter, but also their patron. Some turned to religious allegorical subjects, like The Nun, The Monk, and their Baby (right), a piece of Elizabethan anti-Catholic propaganda, and others to portraiture, like the 1562 portrait of Frances, Lady Cope (right), a sister of Sir Rowland Lytton, and one of Elizabeth's favourites.

It was at this time that it became fashionable to hang portraits and paintings on the wall. Diana, the Huntress (below right), by Frans Floris, is thought to be modeled on Queen Elizabeth herself. Another version of this picture is at Hatfield House, so it was clearly one of her favourites.

From this room, there is a good view of St Mary's Church, albeit surrounded by Mrs Bulwer Lytton's trees, and of Sir Henry Chauncy's *'most lovely prospect to the East'*, now somewhat altered by the Glaxo Smith Klein's Research and Development Centre, part of Stevenage New Town, and the new Great North Road, the A1(M) motorway.

The bathroom adjacent to the Queen Elizabeth room was used by Noel Gallagher when Oasis played Knebworth in 1996

David and Chryssie Lytton Cobbold, by June Mendoza

THE RED
PASSAGE HALL

The 1970s ushered in a new age for Knebworth. The fantasy gothic castle that had been designed to look old in the 1840s, was now genuinely crumbling. In an effort to stem mounting repair bills David and Chryssie Lytton Cobbold opened Knebworth park as a leisure venue and in doing so created not only a much loved summer visitor attraction, but also the premier rock concert venue in the country.

The gates open and people pour in to see the Rolling Stones at Knebworth in 1976

The average English man or woman under the age of seventy can be dated by which Knebworth concert they attended in their youth. Over 100 major artists have played Knebworth since 1974, in front of over two million fans. Three generations have grown up with the name Knebworth synonymous with live music.

Led Zeppelin played their last ever British concerts at Knebworth in 1979. Queen played their last ever concert with Freddie Mercury at Knebworth in 1986. In 1990 almost every major British rock act played in aid of the Nordoff Robbins charity at a one-day event that was beamed worldwide by MTV. In the mid 90s, Oasis gave Britpop its defining weekend with their two record-breaking nights at Knebworth. Then in 2003, records were broken again when Robbie Williams played to

375,000 people over three nights and subsequently released Robbie Williams: Live at Knebworth, the fastest-selling live album in UK chart history and biggest selling music DVD of all time. Memorabilia collected from these shows now takes its place alongside the Byron, Dickens and Churchill memorabilia on display in Knebworth House.

Courtesy of Queen Productions Ltd.

Queen's helicopter arrives above the crowd at Knebworth in 1986

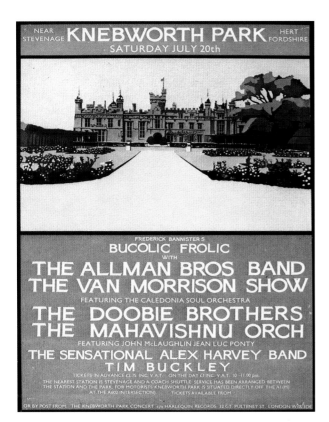

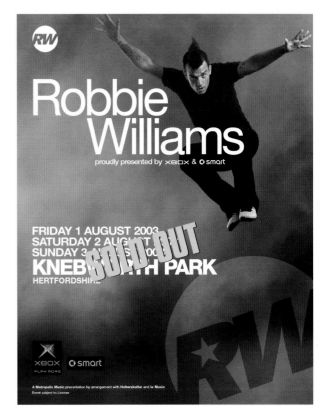

30 Years of Knebworth Concerts. . .

1974 THE BUCOLIC FROLIC:
The Allman Brothers, The Van Morrison Show,
The Doobie Brothers, The Mahavishnu Orchestra,
The Sensational Alex Harvey Band, Tim Buckley.
Attendance: 60,000

1975 KNEBWORTH PARK:
Pink Floyd, The Steve Miller Band, Captain Beefheart,
Roy Harper, Linda Lewis.
Attendance: 80,000

1976 KNEBWORTH FAIR:
The Rolling Stones, 10cc, Hot Tuna, Lynyrd Skynyrd,
Todd Rundgren, The Don Harrison Band
Attendance: 100,000

1978 A MIDSUMMER NIGHT'S DREAM:
Genesis, Jefferson Starship, Tom Petty, Devo, Brand X,
Atlanta Rhythm Section
Attendance: 60,000

1978 OH GOD NOT ANOTHER BORING OLD KNEBWORTH!:
Frank Zappa, The Tubes, Peter Gabriel, Boomtown Rats,
Rockpile, Wilko Johnson's Solid Senders
Attendance: 45,000

1979 KNEBWORTH FESTIVAL:
Led Zeppelin, The New Barbarians, Todd Rundgren,
Southside Johnny, Marshall Tucker, Commander Cody,
Chas & Dave, Fairport Convention.
Attendance: 200,000 over two Saturdays

1980 KNEBWORTH 80:
The Beach Boys, Santana, Mike Oldfield,
Elkie Brooks, Lindisfarne, The Blues Band.
Attendance: 45,000

1981/2 THE JAZZ YEARS:
Ella Fitzgerald, Ray Charles, Chuck Berry,
Muddy Waters, Sarah Vaughan, BB King, Jimmy Cliff,
Dizzy Gillespie, Benny Goodman, Lionel Hampton,
and many many more. . .
Attendance: 50,000 over a few days

Two Knebworth concert posters, spanning 30 years - The Bucolic Frolic in 1974 and the record breaking Robbie Williams concert in 2003

1982/3 THE GREENBELT YEARS:
Cliff Richard, etc.
Attendance: 65,000

1985 THE RETURN OF THE KNEBWORTH FAIR:
Deep Purple, Scorpions, Meat Loaf, UFO, Blackfoot, Mountain, Mama's Boys, Alaska
Attendance: 80,000

1986 IT'S A KIND OF MAGIC:
Queen, Status Quo, Big Country, Belouis Some
Attendance: 120,000

1990 KNEBWORTH 90:
Pink Floyd, Paul McCartney, Mark Knopfler, Eric Clapton, Elton John, Genesis, Robert Plant & Jimmy Page, Cliff Richard, Status Quo, Tears for Fears
Attendance: 120,000

1992 GENESIS AT KNEBWORTH:
Genesis, The Saw Doctors, Lisa Stansfield
Attendance: 90,000

1996 OASIS:
Oasis, Prodigy, Manic Street Preachers, Ocean Colour Scene, Charlatans, Cast, Chemical Brothers, Kula Shaker, Bootleg Beatles.
Attendance: 250,000 over two consecutive nights

2001 MINISTRY OF SOUND:
Jamiroquai, and nine marquees featuring dance DJs
Attendance: 35,000

2003 ROBBIE WILLIAMS:
Robbie Williams, Moby, Ash, Kelly Osbourne, The Darkness
Attendance: 375,000 over three consecutive nights

THE RED PASSAGE AND BACK STAIRCASE

Visitors return to the Entrance Hall via the Red Passage, which was part of Lutyens' alterations, and the Back Staircase, which was part of the original Tudor house.

On display in the staircase are posters from some of the feature films shot at Knebworth, including Batman (1989), The Shooting Party (1984) and Haunted Honeymoon (1986). The house has been a popular location for both film and television, with its rooms representing so many different historic periods and its rare gothic exterior suiting thrillers and mysteries. Knebworth is not only close to major film studios at Elstree and Pinewood, but it is also exactly 30 miles from Marble Arch, which used to be union limit for a day's work, and so could be argued both ways, depending on the producer's agenda.

At the foot of the stairs is a display showing the transformation that the house underwent to become the venue for Warner Brothers' international press launch of the first Harry Potter film, Harry Potter and the Philosopher's Stone (2001). Usually the concern when the house is transformed by a film company is that family heirlooms will mistakenly find their way into the prop truck. In this case the concern was that the — much more valuable — Harry Potter props would mistakenly be left with the heirlooms.

The picture clock set in an early 19th century French painting

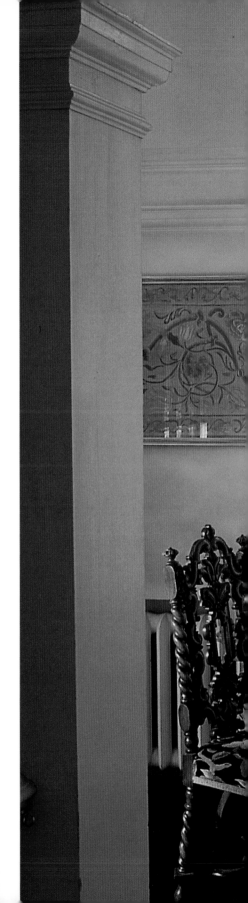

THE INDIAN EXHIBITION

A special exhibition of the Lytton family's connection with India, is housed in the former squash court, alongside the archway in the front courtyard.

The exhibition was put together to mark the centenary of the great Delhi Durbar of 1877, when Queen Victoria was proclaimed Empress of India by her Viceroy, Robert, 1st Earl of Lytton. Described by The Times as '*a staggering collection*', the exhibition contains unique treasures, photographs, robes and mementoes from the Lytton family's time in India. It covers the Viceregal period of the 1870s, the friendship of Winston Churchill and Pamela Plowden in the 1890s and Victor, 2nd Earl of Lytton's period as Governor of Bengal and acting Viceroy in the 1920s, at which time, New Delhi was being built under the direction of his brother-in-law, Sir Edwin Lutyens.

The exhibition includes a 15 minute audio-visual presentation, written by Lord Cobbold that puts the British Raj and Lytton family involvement into the perspective of Indian history.

An Indian statue of Ganesh the Hindu elephant God

The Viceroy's banner pole from the Delhi Durbar of 1877

EDWARD ROBERT BARON LYTTON OF KNEBWORTH VICEROY OF INDIA.

St. Mary's Church

The church dates from about 1120, with the west tower added in about 1420 by Sir John Hotoft, who was grandfather to Sir Robert Lytton.

The north chapel is filled with monuments to the Lytton family. The three early eighteenth-century tombs are amoungst the finest in the country and commemorate Sir William Lytton (*d.*1705), Sir George Strode, (*d.*1707) and Lytton Strode Lytton (*d.*1710).

Knebworth House Education and Preservation Trust

"To preserve conserve restore and maintain for the educational and aesthetic benefit of the public now and in the future the Mansion known as Knebworth House Knebworth in the County of Hertford its historically associated chattels muniments and other contents the surrounding gardens outbuildings forest and parkland including neighbouring buildings of historic social aesthetic and architectural association with the Mansion in particular St Mary's Church the Mausoleum the Manor and Lodge Barns in Knebworth Park."

(extract from the Trust's constitution)

Schoolchildren on a Tudor Treasure Trail for which Knebworth won a Sandford Heritage Education Award in 2002 (below)

Students from the University of Calgary in Canada performing Edward Bulwer Lytton's "The Lady of Lyons" in the Banqueting Hall in 2003

It takes more than a breath to say it, and it took more than a few years to set it up, but in 1984 Knebworth House was given a new lease of life by the creation of the Knebworth House Education and Preservation Trust. With the support of the local authorities the Lytton Cobbold family were able to raise an endowment that they gifted, along with a long lease on the house and gardens, to the charitable trust. In the years that have followed the Trust has made a major contribution to urgent repairs and the general restoration of the house and gardens. It has also made available many of the resources of the house and gardens for education, and students of all ages continue to benefit.

The Trust is a fine example of how cooperation between local authorities and private owners can help preserve the national heritage. However the Trust's present endowment is insufficient to complete the backlog of urgent repairs and much of the political discussion of twenty-five years ago still goes on today.

THE GARDENS
AND PARK

THE GARDENS

There have been gardens at Knebworth House since at least the 17th century, but the present layout dates largely from the Victorian and Edwardian eras.

As he did with much of the interior of the house, Sir Edwin Lutyens simplified the Victorian garden in the first decade of the 20th century. The ornate beds and statuary were consolidated around a tall yew hedge at the back of the garden and replaced outside the house with lawns and the distinctive avenues of pollarded lime trees.

The *"quincunx"*, or five circled, herb garden was designed for Knebworth by Lutyens' associate Gertrude Jekyll in 1907, but not actually laid out until 1982. Other new additions include a walled garden - developed as an organic kitchen garden - and a cedar gazebo that is licenced for civil wedding ceremonies.

Victorian elements do remain, notably the maze that was reinstated in child-friendly box and yew in 1995, and the pet cemetery that is still the final resting place of beloved Lytton family pets.

Lord Cobbold's daugher Rosina, marries Demian Dorelli in the cedar gazebo in 2003 and (right), a general view of the happy occasion

Knebworth House and gardens in the 1880s

19

KNEBWORTH HOUSE

A Styracosaurus eating the daffodils

THE DINOSAUR TRAIL

If you go down to the Wilderness Garden today, you're in for a big surprise! Now to be found grazing amongst the rhododendrons and the redwoods are seventy-two life-size dinosaurs. The Dinosaur Trail is the newest addition to the gardens and has been popular for both leisure and school visits. Exploring the woodland paths, children learn about the T-Rex and the Woolly Mammoth and the difference between the teeth of a carnivore and a herbivore.

Woolly mammoths partrolling the wilderness

THE BARNS

Conference and Banqueting Centre

Coinciding with the wider opening of the House and Park in 1971, two 16th century barns were moved from the village to the edge of the Gardens to provide a venue for catering events throughout the year and providing refreshments during the summer season. The Manor Barn was towed on wheels by a traction engine and at the time was the largest building in the country to have been moved intact.

Since then the Barns have become a popular venue for conferences, product launches, private parties, wedding and other ceremonies. During the 1990s the Barns won the Corporate Hospitality Association's *'Venue of the Year'* Award six times. In 2003 a third barn was added to provide a dedicated tea room, now the popular Garden Terrace Room.

THE PARK

"Suddenly we were in open daylight with the great park stretching on either side of us as far as the eye could see. Clumps of majestic trees studded the gentle undulations and green slopes; herds of brown deer were reposing in the shade, with a few wanderers out in the sunshine cropping the cowslips."

The visitor who wrote these words 150 years ago would find Knebworth Park much the same today. For most of the year the Park's rolling hills and ancient chestnut and lime avenues remain a quiet refuge for grazing herds of Red and Sika deer.

In the summer, however, Knebworth becomes a playground of thrills and excitement for all ages. From Easter until the end of September, the Park hosts a number of special event weekends, including concerts, country shows, craft fairs, car rallies and jousting tournaments. Throughout the school holidays, children can run loose amongst the swings, slides and walkways of the Adventure Playground.

Entering the second millennium of its recorded history, Knebworth is unique in its blend of old and new. From Cnebba to Robbie, living museum to live music venue, Knebworth is more than a place in Herts, it's a place in many hearts.